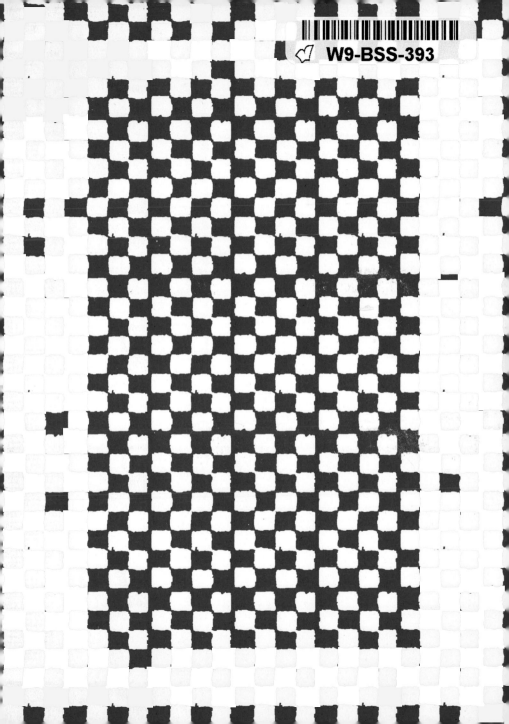

W9-BSS-393

THE
LITTLE
BEAN
COOKBOOK

THE
LITTLE
BEAN
COOKBOOK

BY PATRICIA STAPLEY

ILLUSTRATIONS BY JENNIE OPPENHEIMER

EBURY PRESS
LONDON

For Aaron Jupiter Stapley

First published in Great Britain in 1991 by Ebury Press
an imprint of the Random Century Group
Random Century House
20 Vauxhall Bridge Road
London SW1V 2SA
by arrangement with Crown Publishers, Inc., 201 East 50th Street,
New York, New York 10022

Manufactured in Hong Kong

A catalogue record for this book is available from the British Library.

F Y
PRODUCTIONS

CONTENTS

Introduction	**7**
Black Bean Burgers with the Works	**11**
Navy Bean and Leek Regatta in Pastry Boats	**13**
Savoury Lentil Pâté on Endive	**16**
Venetian Olive and Bean Pasties	**19**
Grecian Lemon Bean Soup with Feta Compli	**21**
Baked Beans with Whisky	**23**
Bean, Cucumber and Watercress Sandwiches	**27**
Chick-pea Fritters with Zesty Pear Salsa	**29**
Shanghai Fiery Bean Lettuce Cups	**33**
Borlotti Bean and Prawn Frittata	**36**
Spice-Fried Bombay Beans with Mango Chutney	**39**
Red Kidney Bean Chilli with Tomatillos	**41**
Mint-Bathed Limas on Radicchio	**44**
Cannellini and Crab Pouches in Roasted Red Pepper Purée	**46**
Chilled Red Bean Borscht	**49**
Mayan Pumpkin and Pinto Bean Stew	**51**
Caviar and Bean Salad de Medici	**54**
Spice Island Calico Beans in Tropical Trenchers	**57**
Golden Bean and Spinach Dumplings on Wild Mushrooms	**59**
Black Bean Soufflé with Orange Liqueur Cream	**62**
Bean Index	**64**

INTRODUCTION

The Little Bean Cookbook is my gift to all health-conscious, taste-conscious and inventive cooks — and to their families and friends. It contains twenty unforgettable main-dish recipes that are centred around the dried bean.

Beans are nutritionally near perfect — a superior source of fibre, and the most protein-rich food in the plant kingdom. Dried beans are the least processed packaged food on the supermarket shelf. They contain neither preservatives nor chemicals.

The thirteen varieties I have used in *The Little Bean Cookbook* are readily available at your local supermarket or health food shop, both in dried and canned form. Canned beans are an excellent substitute for cooked dried beans, so have some on hand for those times when you want to make something wonderful, quickly. Canned tomatoes, too, can be used in place of the fresh tomatoes called for in many of the recipes.

The best way to store beans is in an airtight container in a cool, dry place on your kitchen or pantry shelf. They will keep indefinitely. The longer you store the beans, however, the drier they become and the longer it will take to cook them.

Commercially packaged dried beans should be rinsed before cooking to remove any dust or bits of broken beans. If you are buying them loose from bins, carefully pick through them to remove any grit or other rubbish.

Most people have a favourite way of cooking dried beans. This is my tried-and-true method: Place the dried beans in a saucepan, cover with fresh, cold water, bring the water to the boil, and continue to boil for one minute. Remove the pan from the heat and let it stand for one hour. Now, drain the beans, discard the bean water, and begin again by covering

BLACK KIDNEY   CANNELLINI   BORLOTTI

CHICK-PEA   HARICOT

GREEN LENTIL   LIMA   NAVY

BROWN   PINTO

RED KIDNEY   YELLOW LENTIL   YELLOW SPLIT PEA

the parboiled beans with fresh water and bringing them back to the boil. Reduce the heat, partially cover the pan, and simmer slowly until the beans are soft and tender.

Keep an eye on the beans as they cook. Add more water if the level gets too low — this means the beans are absorbing the water as they simmer. Do not add salt to the beans until they are tender. When salt is added too soon it will harden the outside of the beans, preventing them from softening naturally during the cooking process.

The size of the bean, rather then the variety, determines the length of cooking time. Chick-peas are the largest and will take from two to three hours; cannellini, pinto, red kidney, brown, navy and haricot need to simmer for one and a half to two hours; black kidney beans, borlotti beans and limas take slightly more than an hour; and the smaller split peas and lentils will be cooked until tender in forty to fifty minutes.

Nineteen of the twenty recipes in *The Little Bean Cookbook* begin with precooked and drained beans. When cooking your beans ahead, it is useful to keep in mind that about 225 g (8 oz) dry beans equals about 550 g (1 1/4 lb) cooked beans. Leftover cooked beans will keep well for four or five days in the refrigerator and freeze even better for many months. Plastic freezer bags are perfect for freezing cooked beans, which you can thaw and use as easily as canned.

At the end of each recipe you will find a chart listing the amounts of fibre, fat, cholesterol and calories in each serving. Most recipes also have a "Lean Bean Tip", to help tailor the recipe to saturated fat- or cholesterol-restricted diets, along with nutritional information. Whether you're eating for health or for the sheer enjoyment of it, you will discover that the humble but fabulous bean is a joy to prepare and serve.

Black Bean Burgers with the Works

These scrumptious, spicy burgers are sure to enhance any special event, whether it's after the match, after the theatre, or as a celebration lunch with family and friends. To keep it light and lively, serve the Black Bean Burgers with oven-baked chips sprinkled with salt and red chilli flakes.

Makes Four Burgers

550 g (1 1/4 lb) cooked and drained black kidney beans
1 onion, finely chopped
1/2 red pepper, finely chopped
1 tablespoon diced green chillies
1 teaspoon ground cumin
1 tablespoon toasted sesame seeds
1 tablespoon toasted pumpkin seeds
1 tablespoon toasted sunflower seeds
salt and freshly ground black pepper to taste
2 tablespoons groundnut oil
4 slices Fontina cheese
4 wholemeal hamburger buns
lettuce and tomato, for garnish
8 gherkin slices

Place the black beans in a medium-sized bowl and mash them with a fork until they are smooth, leaving some of the beans intact. Add the chopped onion and red pepper, diced chillies, cumin, sesame seeds, pumpkin seeds, sunflower seeds and the salt and pepper. Mix well. Divide the mixture into four equal parts and form by hand into large, flat patties.

Heat the oil in a frying pan over medium heat. Fry the burgers on one side until browned. Turn the bean burgers over with a large spatula and place a slice of Fontina cheese on top of each one.

The bean burgers are done when the underside is browned and the cheese is soft. Serve them on open wholemeal buns. Top each empty bun half with a tomato slice, a lettuce leaf, and two gherkin slices.

Lean Bean Tip: Omit the Fontina cheese.

Each Lean Bean serving contains:
- FIBRE: 2.5 GRAMS • CHOLESTEROL: 0 MILLIGRAMS
- FAT: 12.5 GRAMS • CALORIES: 298

Navy Bean and Leek Regatta in Pastry Boats

Spectacular in both presentation and flavour, these golden puff pastry boats are stuffed with beans and leeks sumptuously sautéed with fresh sorrel and shallots. The nautically correct will want to serve the entire regatta on a large platter, surrounded by a turbulent sea of blanched baby vegetables.

Makes Eight Pastry Boats (Serves Four)

plain flour
450 g (1 lb) frozen puff pastry, thawed
1 egg
1 teaspoon water
25 g (1 oz) unsalted butter
3 shallots, peeled and finely chopped
2 large leeks, trimmed, well washed and cut into 0.5 cm
    (1/4 inch) slices
25 ml (1 fl oz) chicken stock or water
450 g (1 lb) cooked and drained navy beans
1 small bunch fresh sorrel, well washed with large
    stems removed
salt and freshly ground black pepper to taste

Lightly flour a work surface and roll the puff pastry out to a thickness of 3 mm (1/8 inch). Cut into eight pieces, each approximately 8.5 cm (3 1/2 inches) square. Place the puff pastry squares on an ungreased baking sheet and prick them all over with a fork.

Whisk the egg and one teaspoon of water together. Brush the top of each square with the egg wash. Cover the pastry squares with cling film and refrigerate for at least thirty minutes.

Preheat the oven to 180°C (350°F) mark 4. Bake the pastry until puffed and golden, twenty-five to thirty minutes. While the pastry is baking, melt the butter in a frying pan over moderate heat. Add the shallots and sauté for one minute. Add the leeks and sauté until they soften, about five minutes. Add the chicken stock and simmer until all the liquid has evaporated, about five minutes. Add the beans, sorrel, salt and pepper and cook just long enough to heat through.

Gently separate and remove the top layer of each pastry shell. Fill the crusty "boat bottoms" with the bean and leek mixture and replace the top layer at an angle, allowing the filling to show temptingly. Serve immediately.

Lean Bean Tip: Omit the butter and replace with two tablespoons of extra-virgin olive oil. Omit the yolk from the egg in the egg wash.

Each Lean Bean serving (two pastry boats) contains:
- FIBRE: 2.4 GRAMS • CHOLESTEROL: 30 MILLIGRAMS
- FAT: 15.6 GRAMS • CALORIES: 452

Savoury
Lentil Pâté on
Endive

Savoury Lentil Pâté will shine on those special occasions when you wish to delight the palates of your favourite guests. It may be prepared in advance and served hot or at room temperature, artistically nestling on a bed of curly endive (frisée). For a truly memorable starter, serve the pâté with crusty bread, caviar and champagne.

Makes Nine Single-Slice Servings

225 g (8 oz) finely chopped onions
2 garlic cloves, crushed
50 g (2 oz) butter
4 medium tomatoes, finely chopped
50 g (2 oz) fresh breadcrumbs
450 g (1 lb) cooked and drained lentils
2 tablespoons chopped fresh parsley
2 teaspoons salt
1/2 tablespoon ground cumin
pinch of white pepper
9 to 10 leaves curly endive (frisée)
chopped parsley, for garnish

Preheat the oven to 180°C (350°F) mark 4.

In a large frying pan over medium heat, sauté the onions and garlic in the butter until tender, about five minutes. Remove from the heat.

In a large mixing bowl, combine the tomatoes, breadcrumbs, lentils, parsley, salt, cumin and pepper. Stir in the onion and the garlic sauté. Place the mixture in an ungreased 1-kg (2-lb) loaf tin. Bake for thirty to forty minutes, or until the top is golden.

Let the pâté stand for five minutes before removing it from the tin. When the pâté has cooled, place it on a platter covered with the endive. Cut the loaf into 2.5-cm (1-inch) slices and allow them to lean in a row. Garnish the centre of the sliced pâté with a line of chopped parsley.

Lean Bean Tip: Substitute four tablespoons olive oil for the butter.

Each Lean Bean serving (one slice) contains:
- FIBRE: 2.8 GRAMS • CHOLESTEROL: 0 MILLIGRAMS
- FAT: 2.7 GRAMS • CALORIES: 165

Venetian Olive and Bean Pasties

Create a late-afternoon brunch in rustic Italian style. These flaky, delicate pasties, with their rich, pungent filling, will be the sophisticated and fun-to-eat centrepiece of the event. Complete the relaxed repast with an orange and lettuce salad and a light Chianti. Finish with hazelnut gelato and espresso. *Prego!*

Makes Eight Pasties (Serves Four)

2 tablespoons extra-virgin olive oil
1 medium onion, peeled and thinly sliced
100 g (4 oz) Italian green olives, stoned and coarsely
   chopped
2 ripe tomatoes, finely chopped
550 g (1 1/4 lb) cooked and drained borlotti beans
20 basil leaves, coarsely chopped
salt and freshly ground black pepper to taste
100 g (4 oz) Pecorino Romano cheese, grated
350 g (12 oz) shortcrust pastry
1 large egg yolk beaten with 2 tablespoons water

Heat the oil in a frying pan over medium heat. Add the onion and sauté for five minutes. Add the olives and mix well. Add

19

the tomatoes and continue to cook over medium heat until the tomatoes release their liquid and the mixture thickens slightly. Then add the borlotti beans and the chopped basil. Season with the salt and pepper. Cook for a few more minutes. Remove the mixture from the heat, add the cheese and mix thoroughly. Set aside to cool.

Preheat the oven to 200°C (400°F) mark 6.

Using half the pastry at a time, roll out to a thickness of 3 mm (1/8 inch). Cut the dough into eight circles, using a 12.5-cm (5-inch) round pastry cutter or bowl edge.

Divide the olive and bean filling into eight equal portions, placing each portion on one side of a pastry round. Pick up the empty side of the pastry and, without stretching it, fold it over to form a half-moon shape. Press the edges lightly with a fork to seal the filling inside each pasty. Gently brush the top of each pasty with the egg-yolk wash.

Place the pasties on an ungreased baking sheet and bake them for twenty to twenty-five minutes, or until they are golden brown.

Serve warm or at room temperature.

Lean Bean Tip: Decrease the cheese to 50 g (2 oz). Substitute an egg white for the yolk in the egg wash.

Each Lean Bean serving (two pasties) contains:
- FIBRE: 2.6 GRAMS • CHOLESTEROL: 30 MILLIGRAMS
- FAT: 20 GRAMS • CALORIES: 648

Grecian Lemon Bean Soup with Feta Compli

Prepare to enjoy the most delectable of all Mediterranean soups. Its tart lemon flavour is perfect with the delicate brown beans and sharp feta cheese. Serve this exquisite soup with warm herb bread, a plate of oil-cured black olives and freshly steamed globe artichokes. For the full Mediterranean effect, fill a saucer with olive oil and sprinkle it with black pepper to dip the artichoke leaves in as you eat them.

Makes Six to Eight Servings

1.2 litres (2 pints) chicken stock
100 g (4 oz) raw long-grain rice
550 g (1 1/4 lb) cooked brown beans, cooking water
    reserved
75 g (3 oz) finely chopped chard leaves
salt and freshly ground black pepper to taste
2 egg yolks
4 tablespoons fresh lemon juice
1 lemon, sliced
100 g (4 oz) feta cheese, crumbled, for garnish

Bring the chicken stock to the boil in a saucepan. Add the rice, reduce the heat to a simmer and cover the pan. Cook the rice until it is tender, about fifteen minutes.

Add the brown beans, the cooking water and the chopped chard. Cook for an additional ten minutes. Season with the salt and pepper and remove the pan from the heat.

Whisk the egg yolks and the lemon juice together in a small bowl. Slowly whisk the egg and lemon mixture into the soup. Reheat the soup slowly, stirring it constantly.

Garnish each serving with a lemon slice and crumbled feta cheese over the top.

Lean Bean Tip: Use an egg substitute for the egg yolks.

Each Lean Bean serving contains:

- FIBRE: 2.6 GRAMS • CHOLESTEROL: 12 MILLIGRAMS
- FAT: 3 GRAMS • CALORIES: 168

Baked Beans with Whisky

Baked beans are truly an American classic and a staple at many family festivals. Baked Beans with Whisky is the one-of-a-kind recipe you might find hand-written in a treasured old cookbook. Ideal for early summer picnics, this dish would be especially appetizing with a new potato salad, barbecued corn on the cob and fresh strawberries. Or, you might dress up this dish to serve at a celebration buffet. Simply transfer it to a china tureen and cover the top with a layer of pecan or walnut halves.

Makes Eight Servings

450 g (1 lb) dried haricot beans
1 large onion, peeled and sliced
100 g (4 oz) bacon rashers, rinded
1 tablespoon dry mustard
5 tablespoons dark brown sugar
4 tablespoons molasses
4 whole cloves
1 teaspoon salt
1/2 teaspoon freshly ground black pepper
100 ml (4 fl oz) whisky

Wash and sort the beans.

Preheat the oven to 150°C (300°F) mark 2.

Place the onion and half the bacon in the bottom of a 1.2-litre (2-pint) ovenproof casserole. Add the beans.

In a small bowl, blend the dry mustard, brown sugar, molasses, cloves, salt and pepper to form a thick sauce. Pour over the beans.

Place the remaining bacon on top of the beans and add just enough water to cover all the ingredients. Bake, covered, for six hours, adding water as needed.

After about five hours, or when the beans have become tender, remove the casserole from the oven and stir in the whisky, being careful not to disturb the bacon on top.

Return the casserole to the oven and cook, uncovered, for the final hour, allowing the bacon to become brown and crisp.

Serve the beans hot from the oven or at room temperature. You may prepare this dish ahead and reheat it, if you wish, by returning the casserole to the oven at 180°C (350°F) mark 4 for about thirty minutes.

Lean Bean Tip: Omit the bacon.

Each Lean Bean serving contains:

- FIBRE: 1 GRAM • CHOLESTEROL: 0 MILLIGRAMS
- FAT: .4 GRAMS • CALORIES: 274

Bean, Cucumber and Watercress Sandwiches

Bean, Cucumber and Watercress Sandwiches add a tempting new twist to a traditional teatime favourite. Serve these deliciously filled, delicate morsels at a classic Victorian tea party. The ideal bread for finger sandwiches is homemade and one day old, but any favourite bread with a soft, close-textured crumb will do well. Bean, Cucumber and Watercress Sandwiches can also become the canapé delight of any cocktail party. Use your favourite canapé cutters to shape tempting bite-sized morsels. The tops can be decorated with sliced stuffed olives, strips of anchovy, or pimiento cutouts of hearts, diamonds or Christmas trees. Let your imagination guide you.

Makes Twenty-Four Sandwiches (Serves Four to Six)

1 30-cm (12-inch) cucumber, peeled
salt to taste
550 g (1 1/4 lb) cooked and drained chick-peas
25 g (1 oz) walnuts
1/2 teaspoon grated nutmeg
1 tablespoon brandy
2 tablespoons walnut oil

1 tablespoon lemon juice
white pepper to taste
450-g (1-lb) loaf of thinly sliced bread, crusts removed
   if desired
1 bunch watercress leaves, washed and drained

Slice the cucumber as thinly as possible. Very lightly, salt the slices and leave them to drain in a colander for one hour or so, pressing them from time to time to get rid of the excess juices.

Combine the chick-peas, walnuts, nutmeg, brandy and walnut oil in a food processor or blender and process to a spreadable paste.

Sprinkle the lemon juice and white pepper over the sliced and drained cucumbers.

Spread the bean filling on a slice of bread, layer with the cucumber slices and watercress leaves, and top with a second slice of bread. An average loaf of bread yields about six sand-wiches, which can be cut into twenty-four squares or triangles.

Lean Bean Tip: Omit the walnuts. Use a bread high in fibre.

Each Lean Bean serving (four sandwiches) contains:
- FIBRE: 1.8 GRAMS • CHOLESTEROL: 0 MILLIGRAMS
- FAT: 3.2 GRAMS • CALORIES: 398

Chick-pea Fritters with Zesty Pear Salsa

It is the contrast of a browned, crisp surface with a tender layer beneath that makes these fritters so delicious. The nutlike flavour of the chick-peas surrounded by a crunchy golden crust is a sensational taste experience. Serve with plenty of Zesty Pear Salsa, a side dish of bright green asparagus and a full-bodied red wine. These fritters are very easy to make — ideal for a casual meal with good friends.

Makes Twenty-Four Small Fritters (Serves Four to Six)

450 g (1 lb) cooked and drained chick-peas
1 teaspoon salt
1 medium potato
1 small onion, coarsely grated
1 tablespoon plain flour
2 drops Tabasco sauce
2 eggs, lightly beaten
25 g (1 oz) unsalted butter
2 tablespoons extra-virgin olive oil
Zesty Pear Salsa (recipe follows)

Chop the cooked chick-peas coarsely and season them with the salt.

Peel the potato, grate it, and squeeze out as much of the liquid as possible. In a medium bowl, combine the potato, onion, flour and Tabasco sauce. Mix well to blend. Add the chick-peas and eggs, and mix.

In a large non-stick frying pan, melt the butter in the olive oil over moderate heat. When the oil is hot, drop rounded tablespoons of the mixture into the pan, allowing room for them to spread. Cook over moderately high heat until they are golden brown on the bottom, about four minutes. Turn the fritters over, flatten slightly with a spatula, and cook about two minutes longer.

Serve the fritters on a warmed platter accompanied by the Zesty Pear Salsa.

Lean Bean Tip: Increase eggs to three, but discard the yolks. Omit the butter and increase the olive oil by two tablespoons.

Each Lean Bean serving (five fritters) contains:
- FIBRE: 1 GRAM • CHOLESTEROL: 0 MILLIGRAMS
- FAT: 11 GRAMS • CALORIES: 407

Zesty Pear Salsa

If you prefer your salsa very zesty, add extra spring onions and chillies.

Serves Four to Six

2 plum tomatoes
2 firm pears, peeled, cored and diced into 0.5-cm
  (1/4-inch) pieces
1 tablespoon fresh lemon juice
6 large spring onions, chopped

1 tablespoon finely chopped green chillies
3 tablespoons extra-virgin olive oil
2 tablespoons wine vinegar
1 teaspoon honey

Blanch the tomatoes in a medium saucepan with boiling water for one minute. Rinse them under cold running water to cool, and slip the skins off. Cut the tomatoes in half and scoop out the seeds. Slice them into 0.5-cm (1/4-inch) julienne strips.

In a medium bowl, toss the diced pears with the lemon juice. Add the tomatoes, spring onions and chillies. Mix well.

In another bowl, whisk together the oil, vinegar and honey. Drizzle over the pear mixture and toss to coat. Serve with a slotted spoon to allow most of the juice to drain off.

Shanghai Fiery Bean Lettuce Cups

Fire and ice, this spicy dish is a delight to the senses, and great fun to eat as well. Plan a simple but unique oriental odyssey for your dinner companions. Arrange the Shanghai Fiery Bean Lettuce Cups on a large platter, and accompany them with warm crusty bread. Be sure to use red plates, candles and napkins for that Chinese touch, denoting good luck. Select a dry white wine, perhaps a *fumé blanc*, to soothe the excited palates of your guests, and finish with a cooling ginger-peach sorbet.

Makes Sixteen Lettuce Cups (Serves Four)

2 heads iceberg lettuce
8 dried Chinese black (wood-ear) mushrooms
10 fresh (or canned) water chestnuts, diced
225 g (8 oz) raw prawns
2 teaspoons dry sherry
1 teaspoon soy sauce
1 teaspoon finely chopped fresh ginger
1 tablespoon plus 1/2 teaspoon cornflour
2 tablespoons plus 1/2 teaspoon groundnut oil
2 spring onions, finely chopped

1/2 red pepper, seeded and diced
450 g (1 lb) cooked and drained black kidney beans
50 g (2 oz) toasted pine nuts

SHANGHAI SAUCE

1 tablespoon oyster sauce
2 tablespoons dry sherry
1 tablespoon soy sauce
1 tablespoon Asian sesame oil
1/2 teaspoon sugar
1 teaspoon chilli sauce

Separate the lettuce leaves. Select sixteen palm-sized leaves. Some may need to be trimmed so that they are more evenly rounded. Wash, dry and wrap them in a cloth. Chill for one hour.

Soak the dried mushrooms in hot water until they are soft, about twenty minutes. Drain and squeeze out the excess liquid. Discard the stems and dice the caps. Set aside.

If fresh water chestnuts are being used, peel them before dicing. Canned water chestnuts do not need to be peeled, but be sure to drain them thoroughly. Set aside.

Shell and devein the prawns, then chop finely. Marinate the prawns in sherry, soy sauce, ginger, half a teaspoon of cornflour, and half a teaspoon of groundnut oil. Set aside.

In a small bowl, combine the ingredients for the Shanghai sauce. Set aside. Combine the remaining tablespoon of cornflour with an equal amount of water.

Arrange all the ingredients within easy reach of the cooker.

Heat a wok or large sauté pan over high heat for about thirty seconds. Add the two tablespoons of groundnut oil and quickly swirl to coat the surface of the pan. When the oil just begins to smoke, add the marinated prawns. Stir-fry until they turn white, about two minutes. Immediately add the black mushrooms, water chestnuts, spring onions, red pepper and black beans. Stir-fry for about one minute. Add the pine nuts and the Shanghai Sauce. When the sauce comes to the boil, stir in the cornflour and water mixture. Continue to stir-fry until well blended.

Remove the chilled lettuce cups from the refrigerator. Fill each with a tablespoon of the fiery bean mixture. Serve at once.

Each serving contains:

- FIBRE: 2.2 GRAMS • CHOLESTEROL: 86 MILLIGRAMS
- FAT: 13.4 GRAMS • CALORIES: 457

Borlotti Bean and Prawn Frittata

This colourful Italian-style omelette can be served hot straight from the frying pan for carefree dining. If the frittata is left to cool at room temperature, it can be cut into little squares for a tantalizing appetizer, or into larger wedges for a quick and tasty lunch dish. For the ultimate indulgence, serve the Borlotti Bean and Prawn Frittata for breakfast in bed with a glass of freshly squeezed orange juice.

Makes Four Servings

100 g (4 oz) medium prawns, boiled for 1 minute, then
    peeled and cut in half lengthways
350 g (12 oz) cooked and drained borlotti beans
4 eggs
1 teaspoon finely chopped fresh thyme, or 1/4
    teaspoon dried
2 tablespoons finely chopped fresh parsley
1/4 teaspoon salt
freshly ground black pepper to taste
1/4 teaspoon cayenne pepper
50 g (2 oz) gruyère cheese, grated
1 tablespoon plain breadcrumbs

1 tablespoon extra-virgin olive oil
12 g (1/2 oz) unsalted butter
50 g (2 oz) coarsely chopped rocket leaves

Combine the prawns with the borlotti beans in a bowl.

Beat the eggs, thyme, parsley, salt, pepper and cayenne pepper together in a medium-sized bowl. Add the prawns and the borlotti beans to the egg batter. Set aside.

Combine the cheese and the breadcrumbs in a bowl; toss to combine thoroughly. Set aside.

Preheat the grill. Melt the oil and butter in a 25-cm (10-inch) frying pan over a medium heat. When the butter has stopped foaming, add the rocket and sauté until it wilts, about one minute.

Lower the heat to medium-low and add the egg batter. Cook for three to four minutes, or until the bottom of the frittata is set, but the top is still loose and wet. Remove from the heat and sprinkle the top with the cheese and crumb mixture.

Place the frying pan under the grill and cook until the frittata is golden brown on top, two to three minutes. Transfer to a warm platter or serve straight from the pan.

Lean Bean. Tip: Increase eggs to six, but discard the yolks. Omit the butter and increase the olive oil by one tablespoon.

Each Lean Bean serving contains:

- FIBRE: 2.1 GRAMS • CHOLESTEROL: 63 GRAMS
- FAT: 18.5 GRAMS • CALORIES: 296

Spice-Fried Bombay Beans with Mango Chutney

Indian food, the most aromatic of all cuisines, is distinguished by its captivating fragrances and intriguing flavours. Spice-Fried Bombay Beans with Mango Chutney is a luxurious one-dish meal that will thrill your guests with a culinary journey to enchanted India. Serve the dish simply with a cucumber and yogurt salad, and a large bowl of fragrant basmati rice.

Makes Six Servings

450 g (1 lb) Brussels sprouts
1 large tomato, finely chopped
1 teaspoon lemon juice
2 tablespoons vegetable oil
1 teaspoon black mustard seeds
1/4 teaspoon fenugreek seeds
2 teaspoons chopped garlic
100 g (4 oz) fresh green beans, trimmed and cut into
    2.5-cm (1-inch) pieces
2 teaspoons salt
50 ml (2 fl oz) water
550 g (1 1/4 lb) well-cooked and drained yellow lentils
    (or yellow split peas)

2 tablespoons chopped fresh coriander
mango chutney

Trim the hard stems from each of the Brussels sprouts. Cut a deep 0.5-cm (1/4-inch) cross in the base of each sprout to ensure even cooking.

In a blender or food processor, purée the tomato with the lemon juice.

Heat the vegetable oil in a deep pan over a high heat. Add the mustard seeds and when the seeds turn grey, add the fenugreek seeds. Cook quickly for thirty seconds. Add the garlic and cook for one minute longer. Add the Brussels sprouts and green beans and cook, tossing, for three minutes.

Lower the heat. Add the tomato purée, salt and water. Cover and simmer for twenty minutes more.

Add the cooked lentils, mix and cook for ten to fifteen minutes longer. Remove from the heat and stir in the coriander.

Pour the mixture into a brightly coloured serving bowl. Arrange the mango chutney in a smaller bowl to serve as a sweet condiment to the spicy beans.

Each serving contains:

- FIBRE: 3.6 GRAMS • CHOLESTEROL: 0 MILLIGRAMS
- FAT: 2.8 GRAMS • CALORIES: 117

Red Kidney Bean Chilli with Tomatillos

The engagingly piquant flavour of tomatillos gives this chilli a rich, earthy soul. For a spirited Sunday night supper, set the table colourfully and accompany the chilli with a lettuce salad topped with pomegranate seeds and fresh mango. Warm a basket of fresh corn tortillas and eat them the traditional way: Roll one up, hold it in your hand, and munch it along with the chilli. *Olé!*

Makes Six Servings

one 375-g (13-oz) can tomatillos (Mexican green
    tomatoes), drained
4 whole canned red chillies, drained
3 garlic cloves, peeled and roughly chopped
1 bunch fresh coriander
1/4 teaspoon sugar
1/4 teaspoon salt
4 tablespoons vegetable oil
1 medium onion, chopped
4 medium new potatoes, washed and roughly
    chopped
75 g (3 oz) raw cauliflower florets

550 g (1 1/4 lb) cooked and drained red kidney beans, cooking water reserved
freshly ground black pepper to taste
crème fraîche or soured cream, for garnish

In a blender or food processor, combine the tomatillos (include about two tablespoons of liquid from the can), chillies, garlic, six sprigs of coriander, sugar and salt. Blend to a smooth purée.

Heat two tablespoons of the vegetable oil in a frying pan. Add the purée and cook the sauce for about five minutes, until it has thickened a little and is well seasoned. Set aside.

Heat the remaining two tablespoons of oil in a heavy pan. Add the onion and sauté over medium heat until it begins to soften. Then add the potatoes, cauliflower and kidney beans. Cook another minute. Next add the tomatillo purée, bean cooking water and just enough water to cover. Season with black pepper to taste.

Bring to the boil. Lower the heat, cover, and cook slowly until the potatoes and cauliflower are tender, about thirty minutes.

Spoon the chilli into individual bowls and top each serving with *crème fraîche* or soured cream and a sprig of coriander.

Lean Bean Tip: Omit the *crème fraîche* or soured cream.

Each Lean Bean serving contains:

- FIBRE: 2.1 GRAMS • CHOLESTEROL: 0 MILLIGRAMS
- FAT: 8 GRAMS • CALORIES: 280

Mint-Bathed Limas on Radicchio

Enjoy a light afternoon meal from the American south — one that is succulent and mouth-watering. Set your table where the sun still shines and serve the Mint-Bathed Limas on Radicchio with melon slices, homemade pickles, brandied peaches, a basket of hot buttermilk scones and a refreshing drink.

Makes Four Servings

100 g (4 oz) small tender green beans
salt
1/2 red pepper, chopped
1 head radicchio
550 g (1 1/4 lb) cooked and drained lima beans
2 tablespoons chopped fresh parsley

MINT JULEP DRESSING

4 tablespoons extra-virgin olive oil
4 tablespoons fresh lemon juice
1 tablespoon whisky
2 tablespoons finely chopped fresh mint leaves
pinch of sugar
salt and freshly ground black pepper to taste

With a sharp knife, trim stringy ends off the green beans. Cook in boiling salted water until tender but still somewhat crisp, seven to eight minutes. Drain the beans thoroughly and set aside.

Blanch the red pepper in 100 ml (4 fl oz) boiling water for one to two minutes. Drain and set aside.

In a small bowl, mix all of the ingredients for the Mint Julep dressing, whisking until it has slightly thickened. Set aside.

Separate the radicchio leaves. Rinse, pat dry and set aside.

In a bowl, combine the cooked lima beans, green beans, red pepper and parsley. Toss gently with the Mint Julep Dressing. Arrange the salad on a bed of radicchio and serve at room temperature.

Each serving contains:
- FIBRE: 4.15 GRAMS • CHOLESTEROL: 0 MILLIGRAMS
- FAT: 13.25 GRAMS • CALORIES: 259

Cannellini and Crab Pouches in Roasted Red Pepper Purée

The visual impact of these fabulous little pouches will add that gourmet touch to your next dress-to-kill dinner. All the ingredients — the crêpes, the bean filling and the garlic and roasted red pepper purée can be made ahead of time, and then assembled effortlessly just before dinner. For the simplest elegance, complete your menu with a spinach, fennel and pink grapefruit salad, and a spirited California or German riesling.

Makes Twenty-Four Pouches (Serves Six)

CRÊPES

125 g (4 1/2 oz) plain flour
4 eggs
1/2 teaspoon salt
350 ml (12 fl oz) skimmed milk
60 g (2 1/2 oz) unsalted butter, melted

BEAN FILLING

450 g (1 lb) cooked and drained cannellini beans
175 g (6 oz) crab meat, shredded

12 g (1/2 oz) chopped basil leaves; reserve 2
   tablespoons for garnish
juice of 1 small lemon
zest of 1 small lemon
24 whole chives

GARLIC AND ROASTED RED PEPPER PURÉE

3 medium red peppers
25 g (1 oz) unsalted butter
6 garlic cloves
1/4 teaspoon salt
freshly ground black pepper to taste
3 tablespoons water

Combine the flour, eggs and salt in a mixing bowl. Add the milk slowly, beating to obtain a smooth, thin, velvet-like batter. Just before you cook the crêpes, add one tablespoon of the melted butter and mix well.

Heat a crêpe pan over medium heat. Brush the pan with melted butter and pour in two tablespoons of the batter. Swirl the pan to form a thin crêpe about 11 cm (4 1/2 inches) in diameter. Cook for one minute, then toss and cook the other side for five seconds. Repeat the process, stacking the crêpes one on top of the other. Keep them warm and covered until ready to use.

In a bowl, mix all the bean filling ingredients except the chives. Set aside.

Bring a pan of water to the boil. Blanch the chives for ten seconds in bunches of twelve. Dry them on paper towels.

Fill each crêpe with a scant tablespoon of bean filling. Gather the edges of the crêpe to form a pouch and secure the top by winding it with a chive. Tie the ends together. Arrange the pouches on a plate and cover with a tea towel.

Thoroughly char the skins of the peppers over the open flame of a gas stove or over a high burner on an electric stove, until the flesh softens. Place the peppers in a plastic bag to sweat for ten minutes. Remove the peppers from the bag, peel them, cut them in half, and discard the seeds and stems. Dice the peppers.

Melt the butter in a saucepan. Add the peppers and garlic. Gently sauté until the garlic is soft, but not brown. Add the salt and pepper. Add the water, bring to a simmer, and cook, uncovered, for twenty minutes. Pour the mixture into a food processor or blender and purée the red pepper and garlic.

Place four cannellini pouches on each plate and spoon the sauce around them. Garnish with the remaining two tablespoons of chopped basil.

Lean Bean Tip: Omit the melted butter when cooking the crêpes and instead use a non-stick crêpe pan. Use an egg substitute in the crêpe batter as an alternative to the whole eggs. Substitute the unsalted butter with two tablespoons of extra-virgin olive oil to sauté the red peppers.

Each Lean Bean serving (four pouches) contains:
- FIBRE: 2.4 GRAMS • CHOLESTEROL: 27 MILLIGRAMS
- FAT: 56 GRAMS • CALORIES: 265

Chilled Red Bean Borscht

Chilled Red Bean Borscht is an unexpectedly rich tapestry of colour and flavour. To create a classic European summer meal, serve this bright soup with smoked salmon, dill biscuits and a salad of baby lettuces drizzled with lemon juice and olive oil.

Makes Eight Servings

2 tablespoons extra-virgin olive oil
1 medium onion, finely chopped
3 cloves garlic
4 medium beetroots, peeled and sliced 1 cm
    (1/2 inch) thick
1 red pepper, seeded and cut into 2.5-cm (1-inch) pieces
2 medium carrots, peeled and sliced 1 cm (1/2 inch)
    thick
1.2 litres (2 pints) water
450 g (1 lb) cooked and drained red kidney beans
75 g (3 oz) finely shredded green cabbage
2 tablespoons tomato paste
225 g (8 oz) coarsely chopped plum tomatoes
4 tablespoons lemon juice
salt and freshly ground black pepper to taste

soured cream for garnish
3 tablespoons chopped fresh dill for garnish

Heat the olive oil in a large saucepan. Add the onion and garlic. Cook until golden, then add the beetroot, pepper, carrots and water. Cover and bring to the boil. Reduce the heat and simmer until tender, about thirty minutes. Add the red beans, cabbage and tomato paste. Cook for five minutes. Add the tomatoes, lemon juice, salt and pepper. Simmer for ten minutes.

Transfer the mixture to a food processor or blender, in batches, and purée until smooth.

Refrigerate, covered, for two to three hours, until chilled. Garnish each serving with a dollop of soured cream and a sprinkling of chopped dill.

Lean Bean Tip: Replace the soured cream garnish with plain low-fat yogurt.

Each Lean Bean serving contains:
- FIBRE: 4.3 GRAMS • CHOLESTEROL: 0 MILLIGRAMS
- FAT: 3 GRAMS • CALORIES: 99

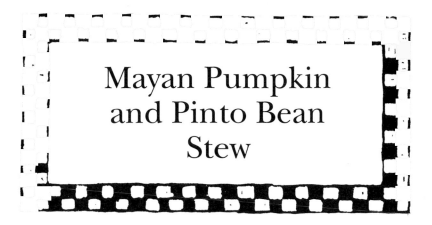

Mayan Pumpkin and Pinto Bean Stew

The Mayans were an innovative people and this hearty stew reflects, in a single dish, all the mystery of the Yucatan and its original inhabitants. Rich in a savoury blend of uncommon flavours, it is a deeply satisfying stew with a surprising, spicy edge. It makes a beautiful, simple meal served with warm tortillas or cornbread, a green salad, and light sweet flan.

Makes Four to Six Servings

1 teaspoon cumin seeds
1 teaspoon dried oregano
1 teaspoon dried coriander
1 teaspoon grated nutmeg
1/2 teaspoon ground cinnamon
3 whole cloves
4 tablespoons extra-virgin olive oil
1 large onion, diced
3 dried chillies, chopped
2 garlic cloves, finely chopped
1 tablespoon paprika
1 teaspoon salt

700 g (1 1/2 lb) cooked and drained pinto beans,
    cooking water reserved
550 g (1 1/4 lb) pumpkin or winter squash, peeled and
    cut into 2.5-cm (1-inch) cubes
450 g (1 lb) ripe tomatoes, peeled, seeded and
    chopped, juice reserved
225 g (8 oz) sweetcorn kernels (from about 3 cobs)
fresh coriander, chopped for garnish

Measure the cumin seeds, oregano, dried coriander, nutmeg, cinnamon and cloves into a mortar or spice grinder and grind thoroughly.

Heat the oil in a wide frying pan and sauté the onion over high heat for 1 minute, then lower the heat to medium. Add the chillies, garlic, ground spices, paprika and salt. Stir well to combine, then add 120 ml (4 fl oz) of the reserved bean water and cook until the onion is soft.

Next add the pumpkin or squash and cook until half-done, about twenty minutes.

Add the tomatoes, corn and beans. Thin the stew with the reserved tomato juice, adding more bean water if necessary to keep all the ingredients covered. Cook until the pumpkin or squash is tender, about twenty minutes more.

Serve the stew in heavy earthenware bowls. Garnish with the chopped coriander.

Each serving contains:
  • FIBRE: 2.6 GRAMS • CHOLESTEROL: 0 MILLIGRAMS
  • FAT: 3.7 GRAMS • CALORIES: 288

Caviar and Bean Salad de Medici

It is rumoured that the first beans cultivated in France were given by Pope Clement VII to his niece Catherine de Medici at the time of her marriage to Henri II. This simple but elegantly festive dish says "celebration", and would be sensational at a country wedding buffet or an informal garden party for dear friends.

Makes Four to Six Servings

3 spring onions
550 g (1 1/4 lb) cooked and drained navy beans
1 hard-boiled egg, finely chopped
2 tablespoons caviar, black or red (or a combination of both)
2 teaspoons extra-virgin olive oil
1 teaspoon lemon juice
1 teaspoon lemon zest
parsley, chopped for garnish

Note: The navy beans should not be overcooked and must be thoroughly drained. This is important, since the caviar will not blend evenly if the beans are mushy or too moist. The beans should be at room temperature before you begin.

Finely chop the spring onions, including some of the tops. In a medium bowl, mix the beans, onions and finely chopped egg. Add the caviar, olive oil, lemon juice and lemon zest. Toss gently to avoid bruising the caviar.

The salad may be served at room temperature or prepared in advance and chilled. For a buffet serving, transfer the mixture to a decorative shallow serving dish and garnish with a small amount of chopped fresh parsley. For an individual serving, arrange a palm-sized, bright-red radicchio leaf on a small plate and spoon the bean salad inside. Sprinkle a line of chopped parsley across the top.

Lean Bean Tip: Omit the yolk of the egg.

Each Lean Bean serving contains:

> • FIBRE: 3.4 GRAMS • CHOLESTEROL: 8.3 MILLIGRAMS
> • FAT: 1.7 GRAMS • CALORIES: 128

Spice Island Calico Beans in Tropical Trenchers

Scooped-out papaya halves become colourful trenchers when they are filled with mounds of spicy beans. For the festive calico effect, you'll want to mix your beans for colour and texture. Experiment with combinations of red, white, brown, navy, black, pinto, chick-peas, yellow or green split peas, limas, or whatever beans you have on hand. Serve the trenchers with cornbread and Jamaican rum drinks.

Makes Six Servings

3 green (underripe) papayas, seeded and cut in half
    lengthways
2 tablespoons extra-virgin olive oil
1 medium onion, finely chopped
2 garlic cloves, finely chopped
1/2 red pepper, seeded and finely chopped
4 plum tomatoes, peeled, seeded and chopped
1 teaspoon finely chopped hot chillies
550 g (1 1/4 lb) cooked and drained beans (use an
    assortment of 3 or more of your favourite beans,
    cooked together)
salt and freshly ground black pepper to taste
4 tablespoons grated Parmesan cheese

Preheat the oven to 180°C (350°F) mark 4.

Prepare the six trenchers by cutting the papayas in half lengthways and removing the seeds. Set aside.

In a heavy frying pan, heat the olive oil over moderate heat. Add the onion and garlic, stirring frequently. Cook for five minutes, until they are soft and transparent but not brown. Add the red pepper and cook until it begins to soften. Add the tomatoes and chillies. Cook, stirring occasionally, until most of the liquid in the pan has evaporated. Add the cooked beans and season with salt and pepper to taste.

Spoon the filling into the papaya trenchers. Place them side by side in a shallow roasting pan. Sprinkle the top of each with cheese. Set the pan in the middle of the oven, and pour in enough boiling water to reach about 2.5 cm (1 inch) up the sides of the papayas. Bake for one hour or until the papaya shows no resistance when pierced with a knife.

Each serving (one papaya trencher) contains:
- FIBRE: 1.4 GRAMS • CHOLESTEROL: 33 MILLIGRAMS
  - FAT: 3 GRAMS • CALORIES: 229

Golden Bean and Spinach Dumplings on Wild Mushrooms

The flavour is decidedly Italian but the presentation is *haute cuisine*. When your favourite mushrooms come into season — especially chanterelles or porcini — assemble a rustic feast around these Golden Bean and Spinach Dumplings. Serve them with a rocket and radicchio salad, very crusty Italian bread, and a deep, rich Italian red wine.

Makes Twenty-Four Dumplings (Serves Four to Six)

450 g (1 lb) cooked and drained cannellini beans
1 small onion, finely chopped
3 tablespoons extra-virgin olive oil
75 g (3 oz) finely chopped spinach
1 tablespoon finely chopped fresh coriander
60 g (2 1/2 oz) cornmeal
100 g (4 oz) grated Pecorino Romano cheese
1/2 teaspoon freshly ground black pepper
1/2 teaspoon grated nutmeg
1 egg white
16 to 24 fresh (or dried) wild mushrooms, such as
    chanterelles, porcini or morels
50 g (2 oz) unsalted butter

salt and freshly ground black pepper to taste
2 garlic cloves, finely chopped

Purée the cannellini beans in a food processor or blender.

Sauté the chopped onion in two tablespoons of olive oil over moderate heat until soft, about two minutes. Add the bean purée and cook for one minute. Add the chopped spinach and coriander. Cook for an additional one to two minutes.

Transfer the dumpling mixture to a bowl. Add the cornmeal and mix well. Then add half the grated cheese and the pepper, nutmeg and egg white. Combine thoroughly.

Preheat the oven to 180°C (350°F) mark 4.

Bring 3.5 litres (6 pints) salted water to the boil in a saucepan.

Coat a large baking dish with the remaining one tablespoon of olive oil.

Dip a teaspoon in cool water. Fill the wet spoon with batter and drop the dumpling into the saucepan of boiling water. Continue this process until all of the dumpling batter is used. When the water in the saucepan returns to the boil, cover and simmer the dumplings for two to three minutes. Remove them from the saucepan with a slotted spoon, and transfer them to the oiled baking dish. Sprinkle the tops of the dumplings with the remaining grated cheese and bake for ten minutes.

If you are using fresh wild mushrooms, clean them with a soft brush or cloth. If the mushrooms are dried, reconstitute them by soaking them in tepid water for twenty minutes to one hour. Drain thoroughly, squeezing out any excess liquid. Slice the mushrooms into rather large pieces. If the stems are shrivelled or pulpy, discard them.

Cook the mushrooms in two batches; if they are crowded in the pan, they will steam instead of sauté. To cook the first batch, heat 25 g (1 oz) butter in a wide frying pan. Add eight to twelve mushrooms and sauté them over high heat for about two minutes. When they begin to lose their juices, season with salt, pepper and half the garlic. Cook for another few minutes, or until the garlic turns soft. Take the first batch of mushrooms out of the frying pan and place on a warm plate. Repeat this procedure for the remaining mushrooms and garlic.

Select a large platter and cover it with a bed of wild mushrooms. Arrange the bean and spinach dumplings on top. Serve immediately.

Lean Bean Tip: Decrease the cheese to 50 g (2 oz). Sauté the mushrooms in olive oil, instead of unsalted butter.

Each Lean Bean serving (five dumplings) contains:
- FIBRE: 7.5 GRAMS • CHOLESTEROL: 28 MILLIGRAMS
- FAT: 26 GRAMS • CALORIES: 407

Black Bean Soufflé with Orange Liqueur Cream

Add a dash of panache to your party to end all parties. Your very happy guests will not soon forget this sumptuous soufflé, enhanced with a rich, tangy orange liqueur cream. Serve it with a platter of baby vegetables marinated in balsamic vinegar, olive oil and fresh basil. And, of course, what is a soufflé without champagne?

Makes Four Servings

450 g (1 lb) cooked and drained black kidney beans
1 tablespoon finely chopped mint leaves
1 tablespoon grated orange peel
1/4 teaspoon salt
5 egg whites, beaten until stiff
300 ml (1/2 pint) plain yogurt
2 tablespoons orange liqueur

Preheat the oven to 180°C (350°F) mark 4.

Purée the black beans in a food mill or blender with the mint, orange peel and salt. Transfer to a bowl.

Delicately fold the beaten egg whites into the bean purée, a quarter at a time. Turn the mixture into a buttered 1.2-litre (2-pint) soufflé dish, leaving a space of at least 3 cm

(1 1/4 inches) between the top of the mixture and the rim of the dish.

Bake for thirty-five to forty-five minutes, until the soufflé rises to the top of the dish and turns a golden brown. Remove from the oven and top with a sauce made by whipping the yogurt with the orange liqueur.

Serve the soufflé immediately.

Lean Bean Tip: Use low-fat yogurt in the cream sauce.

Each Lean Bean serving contains:

- FIBRE: 1.4 GRAMS • CHOLESTEROL: 3 MILLIGRAMS
- FAT: 1.2 GRAMS • CALORIES: 148

Bean Index

BLACK KIDNEY
Black Bean Burgers with the Works 11
Shanghai Fiery Bean Lettuce Cups 33
Spice Island Calico Beans in Tropical Trenchers 57
Black Bean Soufflé with Orange Liqueur Cream............................62
BORLOTTI
Venetian Olive and Bean Pasties..19
Borlotti Bean and Prawn Frittata 36
Spice Island Calico Beans in Tropical Trenchers 57
BROWN
Grecian Lemon Bean Soup with Feta Compli..................................21
Spice Island Calico Beans in Tropical Trenchers 57
CANNELLINI
Cannellini and Crab Pouches in Roasted Red Pepper Purée 46
Spice Island Calico Beans in Tropical Trenchers 57
Golden Bean and Spinach Dumplings on Wild Mushrooms...........59
CHICK-PEA
Bean, Cucumber and Watercress Sandwiches...................................27
Chick-pea Fritters with Zesty Pear Salsa...29
Spice Island Calico Beans in Tropical Trenchers 57
GREEN LENTIL
Savoury Lentil Pâté on Endive 16
HARICOT
Baked Beans with Whisky 23
Spice Island Calico Beans in Tropical Trenchers 57
LIMA
Mint-Bathed Limas on Radicchio..44
Spice Island Calico Beans in Tropical Trenchers 57
NAVY
Navy Bean and Leek Regatta in Pastry Boats...................................13
Caviar and Bean Salad de Medici...54
Spice Island Calico Beans in Tropical Trenchers 57
PINTO
Mayan Pumpkin and Pinto Bean Stew..51
RED KIDNEY
Red Kidney Bean Chilli with Tomatillos...41
Chilled Red Bean Borscht 49
Spice Island Calico Beans in Tropical Trenchers 57
YELLOW LENTIL
Savory Lentil Pâté on Endive...16
Spice-Fried Bombay Beans with Mango Chutney 39
YELLOW SPLIT PEA
Spice-Fried Bombay Beans with Mango Chutney 39
Spice Island Calico Beans in Tropical Trenchers 57